ALL ABOUT ARACHNIDS
GARDEN SPIDERS

by Becca Becker

Ideas for Parents and Teachers

Pogo Books let children practice reading informational text while introducing them to nonfiction features such as headings, labels, sidebars, maps, and diagrams, as well as a table of contents, glossary, and index.

Carefully leveled text with a strong photo match offers early fluent readers the support they need to succeed.

Before Reading

- "Walk" through the book and point out the various nonfiction features. Ask the student what purpose each feature serves.
- Look at the glossary together. Read and discuss the words.

Read the Book

- Have the child read the book independently.
- Invite them to list questions that arise from reading.

After Reading

- Discuss the child's questions. Talk about how they might find answers to those questions.
- Prompt the child to think more. Ask: Have you ever seen a garden spider? What more would you like to learn about this arachnid?

Pogo Books are published by Jump!
5357 Penn Avenue South
Minneapolis, MN 55419
www.jumplibrary.com

Copyright © 2025 Jump!
International copyright reserved in all countries.
No part of this book may be reproduced in any form without written permission from the publisher.

Library of Congress Cataloging-in-Publication Data

Names: Becker, Becca, author.
Title: Garden spiders / by Becca Becker.
Description: Minneapolis, MN: Jump!, Inc., [2025]
Series: All about arachnids | Includes index.
Audience: Ages 7-10
Identifiers: LCCN 2024039815 (print)
LCCN 2024039816 (ebook)
ISBN 9798892136129 (hardcover)
ISBN 9798892136136 (paperback)
ISBN 9798892136143 (ebook)
Subjects: LCSH: Black and yellow garden spider–
Juvenile literature.
Classification: LCC QL458.42.A7 B43 2025 (print)
LCC QL458.42.A7 (ebook)
DDC 595.4/4–dc23/eng/20241021
LC record available at https://lccn.loc.gov/2024039815
LC ebook record available at https://lccn.loc.gov/2024039816

Editor: Katie Chanez
Designer: Emma Almgren-Bersie

Photo Credits: Chase D'animulls/Shutterstock, cover, 1, 3; GarysFRP/iStock, 4; CathyKeifer/iStock, 5; KeithBishop/iStock, 6-7; Meister Photos/Shutterstock, 8-9 (top), 23; Protasov AN/Shutterstock, 8-9 (bottom), 14; specnaz/Shutterstock, 9; Stephen Farhall/Shutterstock, 10; MRS. NUCH SRIBUANOY/Shutterstock, 11; Malcolm Schuyl/Alamy, 12-13; Nature Picture Library/Alamy, 15; JS Photo/Alamy, 16-17; Chronicle/Alamy, 18-19; blickwinkel/Alamy, 20-21.

Printed in the United States of America at Corporate Graphics in North Mankato, Minnesota.

TABLE OF CONTENTS

CHAPTER 1
In the Garden 4

CHAPTER 2
Spinning Webs 10

CHAPTER 3
Spiderlings 14

ACTIVITIES & TOOLS
Try This! 22
Glossary 23
Index 24
To Learn More 24

CHAPTER 1
IN THE GARDEN

A black and yellow spider crawls in a garden. Silk comes out of its **spinnerets**. It builds a web.

spinnerets

A dragonfly flies into the web. It gets stuck! The spider caught its dinner. What is this **arachnid**? It is a garden spider!

CHAPTER 1

Garden spiders live around the world. They make webs in gardens and grassy areas. That is how they got their name!

DID YOU KNOW?

Some garden spiders spin a white zigzag pattern in the middle of their web. Birds see it. They do not fly into it.

CHAPTER 1

yellow garden spider

banded garden spider

CHAPTER 1

Each garden spider **species** looks different. A yellow garden spider is yellow and black. Its **abdomen** is about one inch (2.5 centimeters) long. Its legs are twice that length!

A banded garden spider has bands, or stripes, on its abdomen and legs. The European garden spider has white spots on its abdomen.

European garden spider

CHAPTER 1

CHAPTER 2
SPINNING WEBS

A garden spider spends hours making its web. When it is finished, the web can be up to two feet (0.6 meters) across!

The web is sticky. **Insects** fly into it. They get stuck! They struggle to get out. This shakes the web.

CHAPTER 2 11

The garden spider cannot see well. It waits in the middle of its web. This is where the lines of silk meet. The spider feels the shaking. It crawls to the **prey**. It wraps it in silk. Then it bites the prey with its fangs. **Venom** turns the prey's insides to liquid. The spider sucks it up. A garden spider eats insects like beetles and wasps.

TAKE A LOOK!

What are the parts of a garden spider? Take a look!

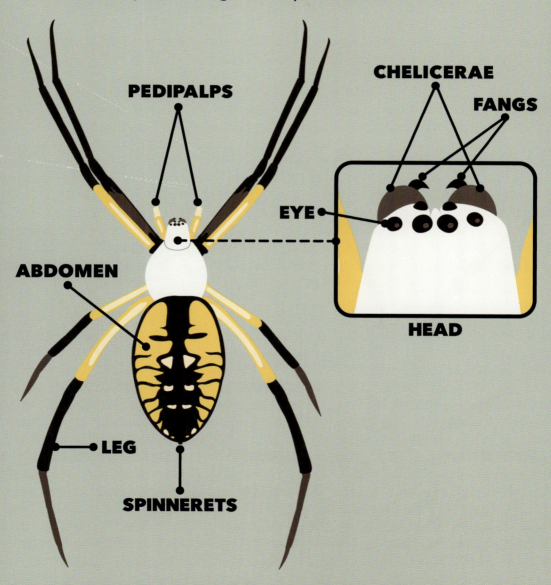

CHAPTER 2

CHAPTER 3
SPIDERLINGS

A male looks for a female to **mate** with. He pulls on her web. This lets the female know he is there.

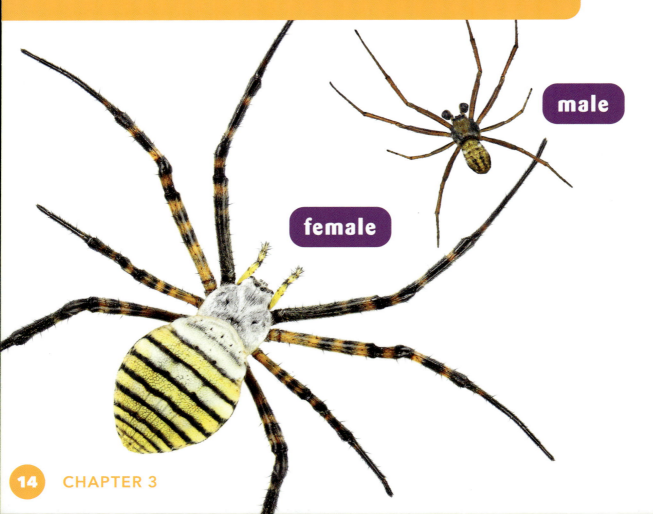

After mating, the female lays hundreds of eggs. She uses silk to wrap them into an egg sac. Then she puts the egg sac on her web. She guards it.

egg sac

CHAPTER 3 15

Spiderlings hatch in fall. If they are in an area with cold winters, they stay in the egg sac. Why? They stay warm. They leave the egg sac in spring when it is warmer.

DID YOU KNOW?

A spider **molts** as it grows. It gets rid of its old **exoskeleton**. A new one hardens around the spider's body.

CHAPTER 3

spiderlings

CHAPTER 3 | 17

Spiderlings leave to find new homes. How? Some let out silk threads. The wind catches the silk and carries the spiderlings away. They land. They look for a good place to spin their own webs.

> **DID YOU KNOW?**
>
> Every night, garden spiders eat part of their webs. Why? They get **nutrients** from any small insects stuck in them.

CHAPTER 3

Garden spiders help the **environment**. They eat grasshoppers, beetles, and other **pests** that hurt gardens. They keep our world healthy and balanced!

CHAPTER 3

ACTIVITIES & TOOLS

TRY THIS!

MAKE A WEB

Make a spiderweb with this fun activity!

What You Need:
- 3 Popsicle sticks
- 1 six-foot (1.8-m) piece of white yarn
- 1 plastic spider
- glue
- scissors

❶ Arrange the Popsicle sticks on top of each other so they make a star shape. Glue them together.

❷ Once the glue dries, wrap the yarn around the center of the Popsicle sticks.

❸ Wrap the yarn around the Popsicle sticks in any pattern you like. The yarn is the silk for your web.

❹ When you run out of space on the Popsicle sticks, tie the rest of the yarn in a knot around the end of a stick. Cut off any extra yarn.

❺ Glue your plastic spider on the web. Now you have a spiderweb!

GLOSSARY

abdomen: The rear section of an arachnid's body.

arachnid: A creature with a body divided into two parts, such as a spider or a scorpion.

environment: The natural surroundings of living things, such as the air, land, or ocean.

exoskeleton: A hard protective or supporting structure on the outside of an arachnid's body.

insects: Small animals with three pairs of legs, one or two pairs of wings, and three main body parts.

mate: To come together to produce babies.

molts: Sheds an outer layer.

nutrients: Substances that animals need to stay strong and healthy.

pests: Insects or other animals that destroy or damage crops, food, or livestock.

prey: Animals hunted by other animals for food.

species: One of the groups into which similar animals and plants are divided.

spiderlings: Baby spiders.

spinnerets: Body parts on a spider that make threads of silk.

venom: Poison.

INDEX

abdomen 9, 13
eggs 15
egg sac 15, 16
environment 20
exoskeleton 16
fangs 12, 13
guards 15
insects 11, 12, 19
mate 14, 15
molts 16
nutrients 19

pests 20
prey 12
shakes 11, 12
silk 4, 12, 15, 19
species 9
spiderlings 16, 19
spinnerets 4, 13
stuck 5, 11, 19
venom 12
web 4, 5, 6, 10, 11, 12, 14, 15, 19
zigzag pattern 6

TO LEARN MORE

Finding more information is as easy as 1, 2, 3.
1. Go to www.factsurfer.com
2. Enter "gardenspiders" into the search box.
3. Choose your book to see a list of websites.

24 ACTIVITIES & TOOLS